The Google Gamble

The CEO's Guide to Traffic, Content and the Mysteries of S.E.O.

by Tim Levy

Updated August 2014

Title: *The Google Gamble*

Subtitle: *The CEO's Guide to Traffic, Content and the Mysteries of S.E.O.*

Author: *Tim Levy*

Published by: *Tim Levy and Associates LLC*

Second Edition, August 2014

Published in the United States of America

Dedication

This book is dedicated to my amazing and lovely family. My life would be incomplete without my Bella, Finn, Zak, Angela as well as Anita, Chris and Nicholas in Australia.

I must also thank my core team and beta-testers who have been so amazing. A special mention goes to Robin, Barbara and Amber.

Finally, thank you to everyone at Vistage, CEOSpace and Secret Knock who have been so important in these recent years.

Thank you, one and all.

Contents

The Google Gamble **15**

   This Book is For CEOs and Entrepreneurs 17

   This Book is About Concepts, Processes and Tools 18

   This Book is Not Technical 19

Traffic **25**

   The Temperature of Traffic 27

      Cold traffic 28

      Warm traffic 29

Hot traffic...30

Traffic Warmers......................................31

Beyond SEO...32

The SEO Game **39**

Fighting SPAM 41

Backlinking can be Evil 42

Article Marketing can be Evil...............44

The Spirit of Good SEO 46

Great Content **51**

Step 1 – Shaping Your Web Site...................52

Awesome Content 54

Human Factors 54

Non-Human Factors 55

Making It Happen................................55

Step 2 – Finding Traffic.............................56

A Cautionary Tale................................56

What to Look Out For 58

The Google Keyword Search Tool Story.....................61

Making It Happen................................63

Step 3 – Great Content 65

On-Page SEO Specifics 66

H1, H2 and H3 Tags 67

Meta-tags 68

A Note on Video 71

A Note on Competition 72

Step 4 – Tracking Your Results 73

Google Analytics 73

Google Web Master Tools 74

Rank Tracking 75

Outsource Everything 81

Hiring an SEO Agency 82

Checking Under the Hood 83

Checking for Bad Backlinking and Articles 84

Checking Impossible Promises 85

Getting Referrals 86

Meeting Local Professionals 87

What to ask an SEO agency or Professional 89

Hiring an SEO Professional 90

An Elance.com Overview 91

Elance.com In Detail 93

    Step 1 – A Free Account.......................................94

    Step 2 – Posting a Job...95

    Step 3 – Picking A Proposal 98

    Step 4 – Hiring and Funding the Job 101

    Step 5 – Doing the Job.......................................101

Frequently Asked Questions 107

Is SEO a one-time thing? 107

Can Graphic Designers do SEO as well? 109

    Something Genuine...112

What is Split Testing?...113

Putting It All Together 119

What are the basic steps, one more time? 120

    Preparation 120

    Step One - Structure...121

    Step Two – Traffic...122

    Step Three - Content 122

    Step Four – Measure...123

End Word + Bonuses..127

   The Bigger Picture..128

   Bonus / Driving Traffic 130

      Sneaky Method One..................................130

      Sneaky Method Two 131

   Bonus / 100% SEO 131

   About the Author...132

Is there more I can do? **136**

THE GOOGLE
GAMBLE

The Google Gamble

The Google Gamble

The Google Gamble is, simply put, the search for traffic through Search Engine Optimization (SEO).

The first and most important thing to know about SEO is that it is a *glorious, wonderful and sometimes high-stakes crap shoot.* It's like going to Las Vegas with your web site, putting a whole bunch of your money into the slots, tables and wheels in the hopes of gambling your way to a fortune. And, like in Las Vegas, no matter how prepared you are and how complex and well tested your system may be, sometimes you win and sometimes you lose.

Even with the best advice or perhaps the help of a kindly professional gamester, Las Vegas is always a gamble! The same holds of SEO: even with the help of a kindly SEO professional or agency, SEO is *always* a gamble.

The art and science of SEO is to understand the rules of the game and its parameters well enough to influence the results. Once you understand the rules you can find out where to put your money, your time and effort in a bid to bring solid *traffic* to your web site despite the unpredictable variables. That's what this book is all about.

And what is traffic? Traffic is when a lovely, interested and genuine person finds and visits your business via your web site with a view to buying your product or service. Aaah, traffic, thou art delicious and wonderful. And Google's very essence is to help you make that match. That's good news, right?

This Book is For CEOs and Entrepreneurs

There are plenty of books and papers out there on SEO. Most of them are highly technical and confusing as they explore specific details of what you should or should not do.

I spend my time working with the CEOs of companies ranging from around $20-$100 million in annual revenue. Simply put, these people don't have the time or inclination to mess around in such a confusing and disturbing swamp of information. They're only after one thing: getting **tangible results** for their business.

That's what this book is about: tangible results for your business. It is designed to give you a fundamental understanding of traffic, content and SEO. It's intended to give you the tools and processes to get this work done quickly and inexpensively.

Let me put that differently. I want to give you the core concepts you'll need to understand what the Google Gamble is all about, what the key factors are and how you might benefit from a mastery of it. Then I'm going to give you the tools you'll need to get those results for yourself and your business without fuss or worry. I'll also do my best to help you avoid the traps and pitfalls that can happen along the way.

This Book is About Concepts, Processes and Tools

I wrote this book because

- I got sick and tired of my clients and friends getting screwed over by disreputable SEO agencies and professionals

- I got very annoyed about the misinformation and hype being marketed to my defenseless clients and friends through dicey web sites, long form sales letters and those funny black and white narrated videos trying to convince you to *buy now!*

As I started to work with my clients and friends, I found that while the fundamental concepts of traffic, content and SEO are easy to understand, very few people knew what was really going on. Furthermore, I found that even when they *did know,* most people didn't have solid steps to take. In short, they didn't know how to *resolve* the situation, leaving their web sites and businesses lonely and under-visited. What a tragedy!

This book, then, is designed to fix those problems. The intention is to give a calm, clear and fundamental understanding of how traffic, content and SEO work and fit together. Furthermore, it's intended to give simple and inexpensive methods to resolve the traffic, content and SEO needs of your business and online presence.

In the end, this book is about giving you the concepts, tools and processes to bring traffic to your business and get your web site hopping!

This Book is Not Technical

You'll notice that I keep backing off in this book when things get too technical. That's because this book is for CEOs and entrepreneurs, not technical people. This book is designed to give you the *understanding* you need to *hire and manage your team* rather than the skills to do it yourself.

For example, let's talk about Google Analytics and Google Web Master Tools. The average CEO shouldn't be spending their time learning these systems. What you want is someone you can trust who has mastered it on your behalf.

It's very similar to the average CEO's relationship with Microsoft Excel. Every CEO has at least a passing familiarity with Excel spreadsheets that run their money. Even if they're non-technical, every CEO should know how to read a profit and loss statement, how to deal with a balance sheet and monitor cash flow.

However, that's as far as it goes. The CEO is not expected to be the technical master of Microsoft Excel itself. Instead, they hire a Chief Financial Officer (CFO) to be *their trusted expert* who works day to day with those spreadsheets and other technical tools to generate high level reports. The CEO manages his or her business in consultation with their CFO, leaving time for other things like overall vision and strategy.

The same idea applies here. I want the CEO to be able to make sense of Google Analytics and Web Master Tools reports without being the technical master of those tools. That way they can see what's ranking and what's not. It takes five minutes a month to monitor your traffic, which is as essential to your business as your profit and loss.

You don't have to be an expert. You just have to know enough to make good decisions.

And *that's* what this book is designed to help you do.

TRAFFIC

The Google Gamble

Traffic

I spend my time working with businesses that have demonstrated long term value in the market place. At first glance, some of these businesses might look boring. While I used to work with big brands, like IBM, Sony, Acer and HP, these days my clients do things like plastics injection mold tooling, child care and legal services. One way or another, my work is about delivering grounded, tangible results with grounded, tangible businesses.

Over the course of decades as a coach and consultant, I've learned a thing or two. I've been able to find some clear patterns for good business.

Here's one golden rule that applies to every business I've ever worked with:

Businesses live and die on traffic.

By traffic I mean *new business leads coming to the door*. Whether they call in, stroll in, click onto your web site or you hunt them down via your sales team, *traffic is critical*. Without traffic you have no customers and without customers you have no business. It's simple, right?

So where do you turn for traffic? You go to Google, the world's largest single source of traffic, and within that, the world's largest potential source of business leads. And if you're talking Google, you're probably talking about SEO.

While SEO is currently being hyped as the be all and end all of the online world, along with its similarly over-hyped step-sister *social media marketing*, it's simply <u>one</u> of many tools you can use to generate traffic.

Let me say that again.

SEO is one of <u>many</u> tools you can use to generate traffic for your business.

It is not the only tool, nor is it necessarily the best tool in many cases. In the end, SEO is simply *one way* to bring traffic to your business. SEO is neither the best way nor the worst way. It's simply one traffic generating tool of many. The great thing about SEO is that you can measure the results easily. If your SEO is not bringing measurable bottom line results, then you're wasting your time and money. And if it's not right for your business, be courageous and use one of the many other tools available to bring traffic to your business.

We'll get to them in a little while.

The Temperature of Traffic

One of the key ways of assessing traffic is by looking at its *temperature*. The temperature of traffic is a reference to how easily that traffic will *convert*. Conversion is when a potential customer becomes an actual customer by buying your product or service. It's the process of taking action to send you some money. If there's no money in the bank, then there's no conversion. I do not consider someone taking you up on a free offer to be conversion; it can be a prelude to conversion but nothing more.

With this in mind, there is a spectrum of traffic – we'll focus on cold, warm and smoking hot traffic.

Cold traffic

Cold traffic is traffic <u>without</u> a relationship. It means that I, the searcher, do not know you, the business. It means that I, the searcher don't even know anyone who has _heard_ of your business – we're total strangers meeting in a dark alley. I don't know whether to trust you or not. Your web site is our conversation as I, the searcher, figure out whether to build a relationship or simply leave, never to return.

SEO can be a great source of cold traffic. If someone types in, "I want to cut my hair," and magically Google sends them to your web page, they don't know you at all. You've never met, so the level of knowledge and therefore trust is minimal. At that point you're a wild card and your chances of conversion are low.

All this potential customer has to go on is your web page. Even with outrageous bonuses and over-the-top guarantees, cold traffic is the hardest to convert. If you're asking them to put their credit card details into your web page, you have created a further barrier to overcome.

Warm traffic

Warm traffic is someone who already knows _about_ you but <u>you probably haven't met in person</u>. It's as if we're meeting through friends in a lovely café, instead of a dark side alley with no-one else around!

So there's at least _some_ kind of relationship there. This person might have been referred to you or your web site by, say, a magazine article from a publication they trust. In this sense, you're leveraging an existing relationship with a person or business this potential customer already knows.

Let's say, for example, that I read an article on how to get a great haircut in Oprah's magazine that mentions your business. Knowing Oprah already, I immediately feel differently about your hairdressing business! Obviously if Oprah thinks your haircuts are great, then by virtue of my trust in Oprah, I probably believe that they truly are. I now transfer that trust and reputation to you and your business.

Now I'm looking to your website to _confirm what I already know_. I've already heard Oprah's opinion about you, so I already think you're kind of interesting. Now I go to your website to confirm that and take a next step, put some money into play and become an actual (as opposed to potential) customer.

Things like blogs, magazine articles, radio interviews, television appearances and media exposure can be helpful to warm traffic in this way. It's all about leveraging the reputation and proof story of that blog, magazine, radio or television show.

This is why people are selling their products through web sites like Amazon. Amazon is an ecosystem they can trust. If your product doesn't turn out to be what I was looking for, I know Amazon will take my side in returning it and getting my money back easily. I trust Amazon to take my credit card details safely, and then make the delivery happen. Ecosystems like Amazon and iTunes are terrific traffic warmers.

Hot traffic

Smoking hot traffic comes, however, as the result of <u>real, long-term relationships</u>. It's the difference between trying to book a romantic dinner with your wife vs. a hot girl you see dancing at the club. One is based on a long term relationship with history and trust. The other is stressful and risky unless you're Tom Cruise.

Relationships, as you know, are formed by a genuine expenditure of energy and focus over time. Relationships occur in conversations between two humans. That usually means face to face contact. Hot traffic might be someone you met and spent time with at a trade show. It might be someone you met and spent time with at a meeting via meetup.com. It's the reason that physical sales forces are still the norm in big business, because they allow the development of long-term, genuine and valuable relationships. It's the reason that branding becomes so important: good branding is about establishing trust.

When you take the time and energy to form a relationship with a human you're generating hot traffic. By the time this potential customer gets to your website, they already know you and your business. This person is poised to become an actual (as opposed to potential) customer. And then, once they've bought from you once and you've earned their trust, they're more likely to buy from again.

Traffic Warmers

Warm traffic can be made hotter by a smoking hot proof story. This means you've established trust by direct and trustworthy testimonials and referrals. You generate further trust when you're certified in some way, such as having qualifications from a reputable source like a college or industry association. You might have other demonstrations of your expertize such as published books, articles in industry journals or exposure in the media. You might be a keynote speaker at a conference. All these things serve to make your warm traffic hot.

Beyond SEO

So here's a quick summary of all those forms of traffic, of which SEO is simply one.

Cold Traffic

- SEO

- Advertising offline and online (including pay-per-click ads and media buys)

- Direct Mail

Warm Traffic

- Blog and Magazine articles

- Radio interviews

- Television interviews

- Affiliate marketing

Hot Traffic

- In person sales forces

- In person meetings such as Meetups, networking and conferences

- In person experiences such as keynote addresses

Traffic Warmers

- Smoking hot proof stories including testimonials and references

- Membership of selective industry associations

- Formal qualifications and certifications from colleges and industry associates

- Personal references (word of mouth)

I personally work with my clients and try to experiment with *as many of these sources of traffic as possible.* I suggest running a balanced blend of traffic sources. It's more expensive to create hotter traffic, but the pay-off is greater because it converts.

Now that you have a bigger picture, let's focus back on the Google Gamble. This book is about using SEO to generate traffic. So let's jump in to the detail.

THE SEO GAME

The Google Gamble

The SEO Game

Let's start with what SEO means. It stands for Search Engine Optimization. To be honest, that acronym means almost nothing and is misleading, so let's ignore it. Moving on.

Instead, let's look at the *spirit* of what it means. Here's the scoop.

Every day, Google runs over *2 billion* searches to over *300 million* people. Crikey. Now *that's* traffic.

What Google is trying to do at any one moment is give each user **the best, most relevant possible search results to their keyword search term**. Google does that by constantly trawling and re-trawling the web to find the best possible web pages, so that it can match them to each keyword search term by means of a sophisticated algorithm (basically, a complicated math formula). This algorithm considers several hundred factors across all the possible matches in an instant to rank your results. Here, a good algorithmic match means a high ranking. A high ranking means you're among the first web pages listed in response to the search term.

The SEO game, then, is to construct your web pages in such a way that Google sees your web page in the best possible light in order to list your page against the search term some random soul types into their search engine. Phew. If that sounds complicated, it's because it is. The part that makes it especially tricky is that *Google isn't telling you precisely what their algorithm is, what the factors are or how they raise or lower your ranking!* It's a secret. Seriously.

So you'll be trying to line up hundreds of factors to get your SEO right. And at a fundamental level, since Google isn't telling you exactly what those factors are, *you're guessing.* That's why I call it the Google Gamble. Welcome to SEO!

Fighting SPAM

And just to make it harder, Google isn't *just* trying to make the best match for the average search user: they're trying to fight the forces of evil at the same time. Maybe I'm being a little dramatic ... these forces aren't exactly evil. Then again, I like being dramatic so let's just go with it.

The forces of evil, in this case, are known as SPAM. SPAM, in this context, basically means *an irrelevant result.* Google is trying for the best, most relevant result. SPAM is everything else. It's that useless web link you clicked on because Google listed it but it turned out to be rubbish. It turned out to be Viagra ads and porn. Have you ever been there?

The forces of evil love to create SPAM that ranks highly on Google but is *not* a good match to your desired search term. These people are also sometimes known as *internet marketers*[1]. OK – that's actually joke. There are, of course, loads of terrific internet marketers. There are also some who are consciously doing things to *game the system* thus fooling Google into listing their pages first.

They often open and operate the very SEO agencies that are enthusiastically hunting your advertising dollar in much the

---

1   Clearly, not all internet marketers are evil! Some are great. The ones that try to manipulate the system, however ...

same way you get good and bad car mechanics. Let me explain.

As you know, a good car mechanic is hard to find. The good ones take honest and true care of your car, tending faithfully to its actual needs. The bad ones prey on your ignorance, charging you sometimes random and fictitious amounts to do work that is not needed. In the worst case, they don't do the work at all, simply pretending to while charging you a fortune. Ouch.

SEO Agencies can be the same. That's why Google dedicates so much of its time to fighting these forces of darkness. It's like Google is Luke Skywalker and SPAM is Darth Vader. Have I gone too far?

SPAM is what happens when someone tries to influence the Google system using skullduggery and trickery. These people have tried to reverse engineer Google's algorithms to influence the rankings dishonestly.

Backlinking can be Evil

For example, you might've heard of *backlinking*. Here's what happened. Google made it known that one of the ways it was assessing your site was to see how many other trusted sites linked to it. If you had lots of these trusted backlinks, they ranked you highly. If not, you moved down in their rankings compared to someone who did.

These SPAMMERS therefore set up fake web pages where they placed essentially fictitious backlinks to the web pages they wanted to rank. These are called *backlink farms*. People were then able to buy *fake* backlinks for their pages. Those pages then moved up in the Google rankings and attracted lots of traffic, based on this lie.

Google, who has a bunch of smart cookies working there, didn't take long to work it out. They, in turn, hunted down the backlink farms. They then systematically discredited or de-indexed everyone who used these backlink farms as well as the farms themselves. This is called being *Google Slapped*. It's graphic terminology, isn't it? Bad luck, you dishonest internet marketers, you.

As you can see, this kind of behavior goes against the spirit of Google's ongoing mission to find you the best, most relevant result.

 Not all backlinking is dishonest. You just have to abide by the Google guidelines, which they've kindly published. Here's a link http:// www.timlevy.net/backlinks or try this QR code

---

Article Marketing can be Evil

Another example you might have heard of is *article marketing*. Here's what happened.

Google made it known that it loves to see articles written about your web pages in high-credibility places around the web that were then linked back to your site. For example, if you had a review of your book on the New York Times web site, a place Google has come to trust (as it should), then they felt your book was probably more important than one that didn't. It would trawl the web looking for articles that reflected glory and respect on your web site.

When that happened naturally, all was well. Google has said this on the matter – *'The best way to get other sites to create relevant links to yours is to create unique, relevant content that can quickly gain popularity in the Internet community. The more useful content you have, the greater the chances someone else will find that content valuable to their readers and link to it.'*

Naturally, SPAMMERS picked up on this and tried to cheat. They created, this time, *article farms* and placed fake articles there to impress Google. So Google updated its algorithm to hunt for obvious duplicate articles, looking to fight this SPAM.

Were the SPAMMERS done? Not likely. Now, the article marketers invented software tools to do something called *article spinning.*

This software would take an article and move the words, phrases, sentences and paragraphs around until it looked like a new article to the Google algorithm. In other words, *article spinning* is designed to deliberately fool Google. Google, in turn, bought up all of the spinning software and reverse engineered the algorithms so it could find the spun articles.

Then, and we're getting predictable now, it hunted down and systematically discredited or de-indexed everyone who used this type of article marketing. Google slaps for everyone. Oops. Bad luck, you dishonest internet marketers, you. Are we getting the picture now?

That's what I mean by fighting the forces of evil, Luke Skywalker style.

 If you want to know what Google thinks, visit the Google Web Master Blog. It's complex and lengthy but you get the truth, straight from the horse's mouth. Try this link - http://www.timlevy.net/googleblog or scan this QR code.

The Spirit of Good SEO

The moral of the story is that good SEO involves playing along with Google's excellent intention of creating high quality content that brings genuine value to the world. You must do so according to the form and structure that Google likes to best influence your rankings. Easy, right?

At the same time, you must know enough to avoid the evil forces of internet marketing. These people will lead you to rack and ruin, also known as being *slapped* by Google. That means that your web site and web pages simply disappear from the Google rankings and your traffic with it. Ouch.

 If you want more detailed information, try Google's own voice on the matter here - http://www.timlevy.net/googlesearch. Here's a QR code to get you there.

GREAT CONTENT

The Google Gamble

Great Content

OK, so now that we know what SEO is all about, what now? How do we go about playing by Google's rules, which happen to reflect a great intention for the good of every user on the web, in such a way that we also maximize traffic for our web site?

There are a few steps you can take. Here's the overview.

- Step 1 – Shaping your web site

- Step 2 – Finding relevant traffic

- Step 3 – Creating genuine and valuable content

- Step 4 – Tracking your results

Step 1 – Shaping Your Web Site

It turns out that while Google is highly secretive about its search algorithm, it does share some guidelines from time to time. The best place to find them, again, is in the Google Web Masters blog – but who has the time?

Instead, we'll take a shortcut.

What internet marketers have found is that Google likes your web site to have a certain form and structure. I'm going to do two things here.

Firstly, I'm going to list out some of this highly desirable form and structure. **Secondly**, I'm going to suggest that you ignore this list and hire someone to do it for you. Simply put, it's complex and ever changing. Nevertheless, you have to get it done.

Here are some of the things Google appears to like right now. Remember, this list is Google's way of looking for genuine value. So please use this information for good and not for evil!

1. **Overall Structure** – sites with About Page, Contact Page, Privacy Policy, Disclaimer and Sitemap. Disclosure page and Terms of Service pages don't hurt either.

2. **Genuine Content** – fresh, unique pages with at least

several hundred words of **valuable** content clearly aligned to the H1, H2 and image tags. What unique means here is that you write this material yourself, each page designed to address a specific issue. Again, this is about providing genuine value and creating something that people will want to read or watch and actually get something out of.

3. **Sitemap Indexed** – if Google doesn't have your sitemap, then you probably don't exist. You post a sitemap via Google Web Master Tools.

4. **Error Free** – make sure your pages are technically correct – that they're w3 compliant and quick. For w3 compliance, try this link - http://www.timlevy.net/w3c

5. **Quick load time** - For speed testing, try this link - http://www.timlevy.net/webspeed

6. **SPAM Free** – sites that aren't filled with stupid ads, stupid links or other distracting rubbish.

7. **Trick Free** – steer clear of unwieldy techniques like over-the-top keyword density, illegal backlinks and illegally spun article marketing. Google is on to you, my friends!

Awesome Content

Google, in their hunt for great content, collects a slew of metrics on your every web page.

Let me restate that in less technical terms. How does Google figure out if you have awesome content? It uses both human and mathematical (non-human) techniques.

Human Factors

Obviously Google's algorithm is a machine, a calculator, so it can't read your content and say, "Ooh, I love it." Instead, Google has hired a massive global workforce to visit your page and make a human choice. They have a 200-page manual that they give to everyone who does this for them, and they pay a lot of people to do this. Every time they visit your page, they have to go through a whole questionnaire, saying in human terms, "Is this any good?" And then rate it. So there's a human factor.

Non-Human Factors

The second is they do their best to do the math. They collect things like –

- Bounce rate – This is the rate at which people enter, then leave the site (bounce) rather than visit other pages within the site.

- Time on site – is the amount of time a user spends on the site, per visit.

- Number of pages visited – is the number of pages people check out before they leave.

Obviously, sites with *low* bounce rates, *high* time on site and *high* number of pages visited do well with Google's algorithm.

So they're doing their best from every angle to figure out if your content is any good.

Making It Happen

As you can see, this is tricky, detailed stuff. I highly recommend you outsource it all and I go over that process in detail in the section called 'Outsource Everything'. So hang in there, we'll get to the *how* in a moment.

Step 2 – Finding Traffic

Again, what is traffic? Traffic is internet marketing jargon for people coming to your web site. Every time Google lists one of your pages in response to someone's search, they call it an *impression*. It means that your web page is coming up in someone's browser when they type in a keyword search term somewhere in the world. That's good but it's only the first step.

The critical next step is when that user, having seen your site listed as a Google search result, actually clicks on your site, jumping over to your page. *That's traffic.* When you have that happen many times every day, *that's good traffic.*

Once you have someone at your site, it's up to you to go from there. That's the topic of *conversion*, which I'll cover in another book on another day.

A Cautionary Tale

OK, so I have to tell you a quick story and it's not pretty. As I mentioned, I spend a lot of time with CEOs. Often times, they're extremely good at something specific like laser cutting or making radios or real-estate. They undoubtedly have their 10,000 hours mastery at whatever their core business is.

What that usually means is that they're generalists at everything else. As a result, they rely on the talent, knowledge and experience of others to get everything else done.

So someone shows up telling them that they need SEO or social media or blog posts or some other random thing done to their site. Once they've heard that enough times, they take the hint and hire someone to get it done.

Unfortunately, they rarely have enough knowledge of what their endgame really is, nor the appropriate tactics to get there.

Remember, the endgame of SEO is bringing highly-qualified, highly-targeted visitors to your web site. That's traffic.

Anyway, back to the story. So this genuine and well-meaning CEO hires someone to *do their SEO*. The only problem is that the SEO expert they hired doesn't care about traffic: they just care about ranking search terms. They don't necessarily care which search terms or whether there is traffic attached. They don't even necessarily care *how* the search terms get ranked. They just want their monthly SEO report to look good for their client. That's the metric by which they demonstrate their value and get paid, oblivious to the results it may or may not generate in that business.

As a result, I've seen CEOs hire so-called SEO experts who use bad techniques like *backlinks, article spinning* and so on. Then Google finds you and you get slapped. Your traffic vanishes.

Oops!

Or, worse, your report shows you're ranking for certain search terms so you think all is well. Only behind the scenes you're wasting your time and money because the search terms have *no traffic*.

Unfortunately, I see this all the time. It's one of the key motivators to writing this book in the first place. It breaks my heart because CEOs pay thousands of dollars every month to be screwed over by evil or ignorant SEO experts. It's the bad mechanic in the car story we spoke about before.

Remember, the *only* metric we care about regarding SEO is traffic. Either genuine prospects are visiting your site or they aren't. End of story.

What to Look Out For

Here's an example of the kind of email that shows up in my inbox from time to time. Personally, I wouldn't hire an SEO Agency from an email like this.

Hi,

I am Rick jones, Business development manager.

We are a Mumbai, India based company.

We provides first page ranking in Google

We offer complete Search Engine Optimization solutions:

On Page Optimization:

1. A detailed keyword research (if necessary)

2. Header text with h1 tag.

3. Write Meta title, Meta description and keywords.

4. Write header text and footer text with right keywords.

5. Optimize alt tag with right keywords.

6. Optimize the body content through appropriate use of keywords in the right place.

7. Modify the footer links

We Use Various Off Page Optimization Techniques

If you are interested reply this mail.

Within 24 Hours we will contact with Quotation & Time Frame to bring your keyword to front page

Kind Regards,

Rick jones

I have changed the name and location so as not to upset this particular company. Everything else is the same. This email came to me on the 8th of May 2013.

OK. Here are some of the red flags.

1. Firstly, it's clear from phrases like 'We provides first page ranking' that these people aren't great with English. Strange **grammatical mistakes** aren't a good sign for a company that has the potential to work with the content on my site.

2. Secondly, it's clear from phrases like 'We provides first page ranking' that these guys are making **promises that they cannot keep**. No-one can *guarantee* first page rankings on Google. More on this later in the section called 'Impossible Promises'

3. Thirdly, from their on-page SEO technique, it's clear they're **not very sophisticated** or up to date. Simply put, they're not telling me that they're doing very much.

4. Fourthly, when they say 'We use various off page optimization techniques' that could mean anything. As we're about to discuss, that can leave you open to **real problems down the line**.

5. Finally, this is **unsolicited email**. It belongs in the SPAM box along with email from Nigerian royalty asking for permission to send me money, Viagra ads and messages from my mother. OK – that was a little joke – I always read messages from my mother!

In the end, this email doesn't really convince me that these guys know what they're talking about. I'd never hire them. More on how to find good SEO resources in the next section.

The Google Keyword Search Tool Story

So how *do* you find traffic? By using free tools like Google's Keyword Search Tool, which is now incorporated into their *Keyword Planner*.

The *good* part about Google is that they'll actually tell you if there's potential traffic for any given search term. The *truly great* part about Google is that they'll also throw up a bunch of options you might not have thought of that may also have traffic. Wow. Nice!

 All you have to do is visit the Google Keyword Search Tool to figure this out. Here's the link – http://www.timlevy.net/keyword - or a QR code to get you there.

I'll explain how this works by telling you a little story. I was working with a CEO in the childcare industry. His web site had a blog post with a great idea for kids at Christmas. The post was titled 'Yummy Reindeer Chow' which was very cheerful.

There was, however, a fatal flaw from the SEO perspective: no traffic.

When we typed 'Yummy Reindeer Chow' into the Google Keyword Search tool, it told us that there were (drumroll, please) ZERO people searching on that term. Seriously. None.

So the blog post became a waste of time and money. No one was searching on it and Google wasn't sending anyone there.

We typed in some other terms that were still clearly descriptive of the page like

- Christmas activity

- Christmas recipe, and

- Christmas treats

The Google Keyword tool them came back to us with not just those three results, but also several hundred further suggestions. Each suggestion was listed with the number of *global monthly searches*. That means the number of times people are actually searching for the term.

The keyword search term 'Christmas activity' gets 60,500 searches. Seriously. That's as many as 60,500 visits to your site you're leaving on the table simply because you titled the blog post ineffectively.

The keyword search term 'Christmas recipe' gets 368,000 searches. Better yet, the Google Keyword Search Tool tells us that the pluralized form of the keyword search term yields even higher. It turns out that 550,000 people are searching on the term 'Christmas recipes' every month. That final 's' is crucial, wouldn't you say?

So if we simply change the title of the blog post to 'Christmas recipes' we get in the game for as many as *half a million visitors per month*. Are you starting to understand why Keyword research is so important?

Making It Happen

Of course, there's more to this kind of research than simply using this one tool. I also like a tool called Market Samurai, for example. The idea is to identify terms that are high traffic and low competition. That's where the magic lies.

With that in mind, I work with people from elance.com or, at a pinch, fiverr.com.

If you go to fiverr.com you'll find the world's largest database of people who will work for you at $5 per task. Seriously.

Once you're there, ignore what's on the front page and type *keyword research* into their search window. There you'll find people who would love to do sophisticated research on your behalf for $5. They'll tell you the best keyword search term to use as your article's title and in the content along with the kind of traffic it can provide.

More on elance.com in the next section.

Step 3 – Great Content

Once you have a series of keyword search terms that actually have potential traffic attached to them, you can go ahead and create valuable content to post onto your site. Google is currently very sympathetic to sites with blog posts about valuable (read genuine) topics.

- If you have a site with existing blog posts, go back and do the research to figure out a new heading or subtle reframing of your topic to optimize traffic.

- If you're creating a site, take the time to generate a list of great keyword search terms to optimize the traffic *before* writing the posts.

Then, just go for broke. With well researched keyword search terms, more posts equals more traffic.

And again – we're focusing on creating material that is genuinely valuable.

In the end, Google will reward you for your great content. Your reward is called Page Ranking (PR). Web sites like the New York Times, for example, have a very high PR. It is a reward for good content over time. Now that their site enjoys high PR, almost anything they post will rank highly on Google.

Anything else is SPAM and everyone, including Google, hates SPAM. So go the extra mile to create something real. Here's the guiding principal:

If you'd take a few minutes out of your day to read it – then it's good.

If you'd click over to something else, then so would everyone else.

On-Page SEO Specifics

It turns out that when you present your content, Google is looking for some specific indicators it calls 'on-page SEO'.

Let me explain this with an example. If you're trying to speak French to a person who only speaks English, they're never going to understand you. You must speak French to a French-speaking person, and English to an English-speaking person. The same applies to Google. You have to speak Google to Google.

Here are some hints regarding simple on-page SEO

1. Make sure you set your H1, H2 and H3 tags

2. Make sure you fill out your meta-tags

H1, H2 and H3 Tags

Let me add some specifics here. Google likes to know that your page is focused on one particular topic. It looks to your **headings** to figure that out.

It works similarly to a simple Microsoft word document. In a simple document, you'll title the page with the style called Heading 1. Then, if you have several sub-headings, you'll set them to be Heading 2. If any of these have sub-headings within them, you'll use the Heading 3 style to mark them out. That way, if you ask Microsoft word to insert an automatic table of contents, it'll already know the import headings, sub-headings and sub-sub-headings to list.

Web pages are the same. The style heading 1 is indicated by what are called H1 tags. Heading level 2 is indicated by H2 tags. Heading level 3 is indicated by H3 tags.

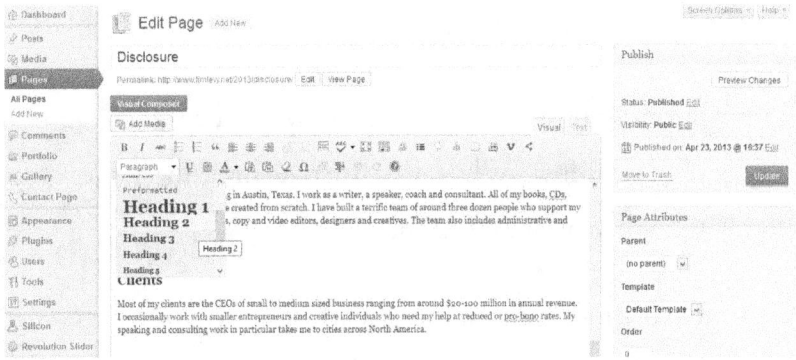

Meta-tags

You've probably heard about meta-tags, so what are they? Meta-tags are tricky for most people to understand because they're invisible on a normal web page. They were designed to be included in the raw html so that Google could search them out behind the scenes, without showing up on the web page that normal users see. Google uses the information associated with those tags to figure out what the page is about and how to rank it within their search algorithm.

These meta-tag codes were usually included in the html header, which is entirely invisible. There are a series of different helpful meta-tags hidden in there including –

- **Meta- description** –a brief description of what the page is about.

- **Meta-keywords** – these are keywords and phrases that you hope to rank for.

- **Title** – this is the copy that shows at the top of the web page window. While this isn't technically a meta-tag, Google pays it attention, too.

- **Excerpt** – this is a quick extract from your page, also describing your content. While it's not technically a meta-tag, Google can pay it attention, too.

So how do you set these? Back in the day you had to master html to do this. These days, using content management systems like WordPress, it's a lot easier. Some of the current WordPress themes include SEO as part of the package. If they don't, you can use free SEO plugins like <u>All in One SEO</u>. Again, I'd let your SEO professional recommend the latest, since it's always changing. I use WordPress themes that include SEO as part of them, so it's already installed and ready to go. WordPress themes are basically the design of your web site. In WordPress you can swap these around at will, changing the look of your site. They sometimes include more sophisticated features like SEO.

Once your theme or plugin is activated, an SEO window will come up underneath your individual WordPress page in the editing area. You simply fill in the meta-tag fields, hit the 'publish' button and you're good to go. Here's a screen shot of how that looks from my own web site.

Again, this book is for CEOs and entrepreneurs, not technical web people. I want to tell you enough to work responsibly with SEO professionals who are either working for you directly or as part of an SEO agency.

 If you'd like some more technical information on meta-tags, try Google's own posting on the matter. Here's the link – http://www.timlevy. net/metatags or the QR code to jump you there.

A Note on Video

If you're using video, which is great, make sure to do these two things:

i. Make sure to create a transcription of your video and attach it as a closed caption for subtitling.

ii. Include that transcript as actual text on the web page below the video.

Why is this so important? It's important because the current Google ranking algorithms *cannot watch your video.* So if you have a video on a page with the best content in the world, it might as well be invisible to Google.

Google can, however, index closed caption content. It can also, of course, index the transcript. So make your videos visible by including both.

And how to get it done? Go to fiverr.com and have someone transcribe your video and create a closed caption file for a measly five bucks. Seriously. Get it done.

A Note on Competition

As we've said from the get go, Google is unpredictable. While you're doing the best research you can to find the best keyword search terms with the most traffic and lowest competition, not everything will rank.

There are some things that Google will allow you to do to promote your posts. Here are some tactics that appear to get results at the moment –

i. you could send out a press release detailing your latest post

ii. you could encourage people to view and like your post via social media

iii. you could encourage bloggers to review and recommend your post

iv. you could drive traffic using brute force methods like pay per click advertising via sites like Google and / or Facebook

Again, you can hire people via elance.com to manage these processes for you. Standby for a whole section on how to do this.

Step 4 – Tracking Your Results

OK. So let's say you've shaped your site in accordance with Google's requirements, you've researched and found some *potential* traffic and you've created genuine and valuable content in response. Well done, you've mastered steps 1, 2 and 3. What now?

Now, you're up to Step 4 which is figuring out if you've actually done any good. Fortunately, while Google won't *tell you jack* about their algorithm itself, they're open communicators when it comes to sharing *the results*. They've set up something called Google Analytics.

Google Analytics

Google Analytics is a free service designed to help you figure out what's working and what's not.

 Here's the link – http://www.timlevy.net/analytics and the QR code.

When you get this free software hooked into your site, Google will keep track of exactly which keyword terms are getting exactly how many visits. They'll even tell you how many impressions they made – which is to say the number of times they were displayed before they were clicked, if they were clicked. They'll tell you how the term is ranking – everything.

There's a minefield of data there, so hire someone who knows SEO to distill it into a helpful report for you every month. All you need is the top line – which search terms brought how much traffic. In other words – is your investment paying off?

You can even set up Google Analytics to track your conversion: again a topic for another book.

Google Web Master Tools

Google has even gone one step further and created something called Google Web Master Tools for the advanced user. It's also free. This is where, for example, you can submit your sitemap directly to Google to make sure they've indexed your pages.

 Here's the link - http://www.timlevy.net/webmaster and the QR code.

This stuff is tricky but critical for the SEO professional.

Rank Tracking

I use another kind of tool, as well. I have something called _rank tracking_ software. That's a fancy way of saying software that keeps track of how many people are getting to your site by means of Google serving up your page in response to a certain search term. This software tracks your traffic over time.

I use something called _Rank Tracker_ for want of a more original name. There are plenty of these around. They provide you with a moment to moment dashboard of search terms, their ranking and traffic in one easy dashboard. I find this easier to use than the Google tools but it's just my preference.

 Here's the link http://www.timlevy.net/rank and the QR code

And just FYI, I'm not affiliated with these guys – so feel free to check them out or find something else.

OUTSOURCE
EVERYTHING

The Google Gamble

Outsource Everything

Now do you see why I outsource everything? The Google Gamble is just too complex for most businesses to master. And why would you want to when you can access these kinds of services so easily and cheaply?

There are two ways to go here:

1. you can outsource to an SEO Agency, or

2. you can work directly with SEO professionals.

Personally, I work directly with the professionals via fiverr.com and elance.com with great results. With the steps outlined in the previous section, you can guide your SEO professional to maximize your results. It takes a little more effort but allows you to manage your team more closely. It's also less expensive in general.

Lots of people and businesses prefer to hire SEO agencies, so let's look into SEO Agencies first.

Hiring an SEO Agency

Many businesses have probably tried to hire an SEO company and been burned by companies that made *big promises but didn't produce.*

Again, Google is on a lifelong mission to hunt down and identify the best content, the best expertise and niche answers to your search questions. Now, while the mission has been constant, the algorithm that they've been using to achieve that goal has been in a constant state of evolution since Day 1. This ever-changing, ever-moving algorithm makes it very difficult to get grounded, consistent results. Basically, *Google is constantly changing its mind.* SEO agencies, therefore, are engaged in a never-ending chase of Google's thoughts. It's endless!

On the plus side, Google has been saying from Day 1, "We want legitimate, awesome content. Don't take shortcuts. Don't goof around, just do great content." When you consistently create great content you'll have the most stable Google experience you can have. Not that any Google experience is inherently stable, but with great content you'll have the best chance.

If you work with an SEO agency therefore, their job should be to simply *make your great content conform to Google's system.* That's it – nothing more. It's imperative that you do not allow them to game the system. As soon as your SEO Agency uses tricks to game the system like illegal backlinking or spun article marketing (to name but two), then you're vulnerable to your very own Google slap.

Checking Under the Hood

So how do you know if your SEO agency is doing the right things? How do you find out if they're doing bad things that could hurt you in the end?

Well, it's similar to working with your auto mechanic in that car story I told earlier. You *check under the hood* to make sure they've done the work they say they've done.

It turns out it's pretty easy to find out.

Checking for Bad Backlinking and Articles

It's easy to get a list of all the backlinks that are currently linking to your site. Here are a few techniques.

1. Go to Google and type in 'link: your URL'. For example, I'd type in 'link: www.timlevy.net' and it'll show me a bunch of backlinks that it's paying attention to right now.

2. Go to Google Web Master Tools, which lists backlinks also.

3. Go to Google and type 'backlink checker' into the engine to find a web site that specializes in this kind of thing.

4. There are also specialized software tools that track backlinks – and now we're getting too technical so I'll stop.

If you get that list and you see backlinks and / or articles from places that are just inexplicable then you know your SEO agency is creating backlink rubbish and potentially trying to game the system. That's bad.

If you see a bunch of links from reputable places that you're aware of, then you're in good shape. Now you can trust your auto mechanic and breathe easy. Good, right?

One backlink that came up for my web site comes from Wikipedia - http://en.wikipedia.org/wiki/Tim_Levy. This is a great backlink because Wikipedia is a trusted source of links in Google's eyes – and in the eyes of the world! This backlink adds authenticity to my web site and helps my rankings. So I'm good.

Checking Impossible Promises

A lot of SEO agencies make *impossible promises* to get a sale. Simply put, it's not possible to promise that you're going to rank a term on Google because it's fundamentally a *gamble.* Even when you do everything right, you're not guaranteed a result. Add to that the fact that Google is constantly upgrading its algorithm and you'll begin to get the picture.

The problem is that these agencies will resort to illegal tactics to meet this impossible promise. They can employ tactics from the dark side to rank your term and that's where you have a formula for disaster. By the way, when I say illegal I don't mean that the police will hunt you down. I'm pretty sure the FBI doesn't care. I'm talking about illegal from Google's point of view. And once Google finds out, you're in danger of paying a price as high as being permanently de-indexed. De-indexing is being thrown out of Google meaning Google will never show your website!

So if an SEO Agency is making promises that sound too good to be true, they probably are. Be sure to check out their tactics and make sure they aren't doing illegal back linking, article marketing or whatever else looks dodgy.

Getting Referrals

A tip to avoid any of these bad practices is to make sure you **get referrals**. Don't just go on the net and Google 'SEO Agency' and hire some random company. Instead, take the time to ask some of your colleagues whom they're using, and what level of measurable results they are getting.

When you get two or three people referring you to the same company, you've likely got someone you can trust. Take the time to find someone with proven results over the course of time. Not just over one month, but over several years.

The questions you're asking potential SEO agencies are things like "What kind of traffic are you getting and how can you prove it to me?"

If they prove it by showing you a conclusive Google Analytics page with impressive statistics on their delivery of SEO traffic that is measurably converting to phone calls, sales leads and direct transactions, then you have a winner. If they can prove a result all the way down to your bottom line, then that's a valuable SEO agency. Anything less is questionable.

Meeting Local Professionals

The other thing that you could do is attend a *meetup*. Meetup. com is a web site that lists local events in your area. By local events, I mean local meetings of *actual humans*. I know this is a crazy idea, since we do everything via texting and email these days. Seriously, though – there are still actual humans out there. There is value in meeting people *in the flesh*. Firstly, they might be nice and buy you dinner. Secondly and more importantly, people are less likely to *lie to your face*.

By meeting in person, you can form relationships and trust. It seems basic but it's worth pointing out.

 Here's a little video I whipped up that explains meetup.com in detail – <u>http://www.timlevy. net/meetup</u> and a QR code to get you there.

To do this, you visit **meetup.com** to find a local event. You can type in the name of your town and then relevant keywords like traffic, SEO, SEM or Internet Marketing. The web site will then bring up all the events happening within a specified radius, when they're on and who is running the group. From that point it's easy to get in touch, get the details and attend. Most Meetups are free.

A lot of the good Meetups have speakers, so you might learn something as well as having a chance to network. There's every chance you'll find the SEO professional of your dreams at a meetup.com event.

For example, I'll do this live online (as I write this) for Austin, Texas. It asks what I'm interested in. I'm interested in SEO. Here's what it brought up:

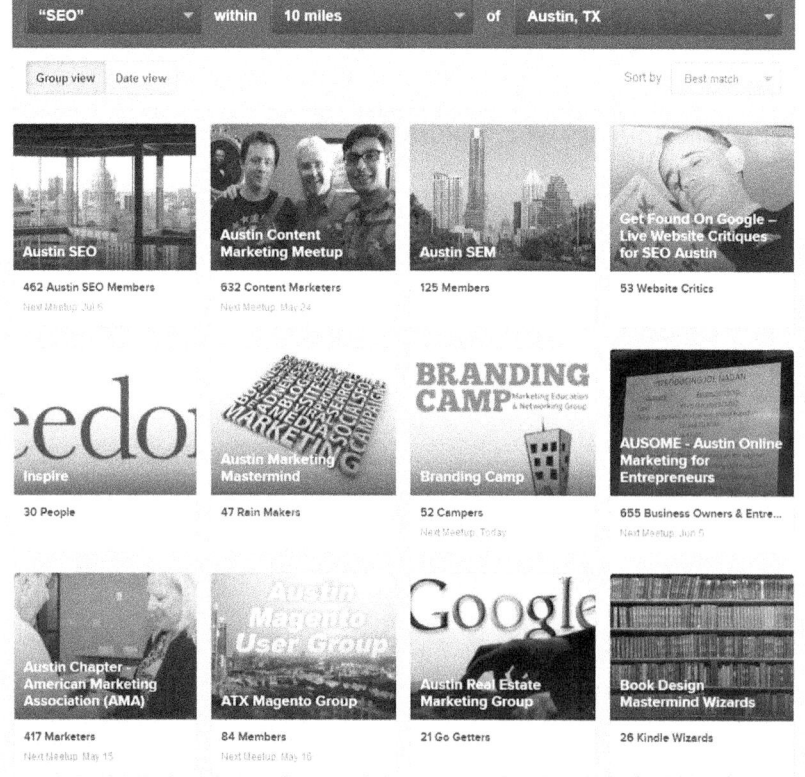

I could go to one of those meet-ups and meet people who are already talking about this and I could get some references or potential hires right then and there.

Also – if you're in Austin, TX – check out the Internet Marketing Party run by my friend David Gonzales. It's full of amazing talent. And again – I have no formal affiliation there – just a genuine recommendation.

What to ask an SEO agency or Professional

So what kinds of questions should you ask an SEO professional or agency, giving them a chance to show off their expertise and tactics?

I would say to them, I'm interested in SEO because I'm interested in traffic. Traffic is the keyword. SEO is just a means to an end. So talk to me about traffic.

I'd ask "*What traffic can you guarantee me or what traffic can we hope to get and what conversion can we hope to get? How warm is the traffic? How likely is it to convert and how can we measure that?*"

If they just say we'll just take a page and SEO and make it rank, then that's pointless. If there's no traffic for that page, then you just ranked yourself for a page with no visitors.

I'd ask *"Tell me what I can hope to get out of this? Tell me the big picture. How many people can I expect to visit my site, and purchase a product or service from my business, that is not already doing so right now?"*

If they don't have a good answer to that, then they're not really serving your big picture agenda, so why would you hire them?

I'd also ask *"Who can I talk to who you've already worked for who can share their experience of working with you and how it's affected the bottom line of their business?"*

And if they're not prepared to give you references, why would you hire them? Go find someone who will.

Hiring an SEO Professional

If you want to hire individuals rather than an agency, you can work through web sites like fiverr.com and Elance.com to find, hire and manage them.

Before we get into that, I want to mention that I've written a book called **the Entrepreneurial Handbook** focusing on building your own team using tools like fiverr.com and Elance.com which contains far more detail. I'm going to include a relevant excerpt below.

 Here's a link to the Entrepreneurial Handbook http://www.timlevy.net/handbook – or a QR code to get you there.

An Elance.com Overview

OK, here's a step by step overview of what you do on elance. com.

i. Go get yourself a **free account**. It costs nothing to join.

ii. **Post a job** asking their enormous worldwide database of people to do whatever you want. In this case, you'll be asking them to do various aspects of your SEO strategy. I recommend splitting it up into manageable pieces. Feel free to cut and paste bits and pieces of this paper to use as your brief.

iii. Now people on elance.com will pitch for your business by sending you their **proposals**. I routinely get 10-20 proposals within two or three days of posting a job. As part of the proposal, these people will *set their own price*. You can now use a variety of elance. com metrics to figure out who is good and who is not. These metrics include

a. A rating system out of 5 stars

b. A money system showing you how much they've earned via Elance

c. A testimonial system listing feedback from past jobs

d. A portfolio system in which they're able to show off past work

iv. I like to take an extra step and **talk** to my final two or three applicants via video Skype. This seems to really sort the wheat from the chaff. It also helps me figure out if I like the person. I only work with people I like.

v. Now you **hire the person** and send the agreed on fee to elance.com. This is key. You don't send the freelancer any money, the money goes into escrow at elance.com directly.

vi. Now, working via the Elance interface, you manage your new team member in **doing the work**.

vii. When the work is done, you **release the funds** from escrow to the freelancer. If you have any problems, you can always ask the team at elance.com to mediate your problems. I've personally never had to resort to this.

And you're done.

I usually pay my elance.com freelancers a matter of a few hundred dollars for any one task. It's a seriously good bargain.

Elance.com In Detail

*Here's a slightly modified excerpt from my book **the Entrepreneurial Handbook** that gives you some more detail on working with Elance.com.*

Elance is the best place I know to find freelancers from all over the world, ready and willing to do a huge a variety of tasks. I use it project by project. If I need something designed, I get it designed by an Elance freelancer. If I need a web site made, I hire an Elance freelancer. If I need help with content or SEO, I hire an Elance freelancer. Are you getting the picture?

By the way, Elance.com is not the only freelance site. There are various competitors, including Odesk and Freelancer. Elance is the one I started with and perhaps it's the world's largest database of freelancers. (Note – at the time of this update, Elance and oDesk are merging)

And just to be super clear, I'm not affiliated with Elance.com in any way. I'm just a fan!

I've hired lots of Elance freelancers. I've hired jobs including: editing books, creative design, web development, online research for business leads, and bookkeeping. It's an incredibly diverse group of people. Have a look at elance.com to see what's happening. When I looked today, I found over 100,000 separate jobs had been posted over the past month, and over $700,000,000 has been made. Yes, that's $700 Million in business. Just browse different sorts of things you can get done here in marketing, consulting, finance, design, and of course, SEO.

Step 1 – A Free Account

The first thing to do is to get a free account. This goes for whether you want to do some work yourself and get paid, or whether you want to get some work done. So get yourself registered. When you're registered, sign in.

When I sign myself in, there will be a security question here just to make sure I am who I say I am.

Here are some examples of the work I have going right now –

- A transcript and edit of a new book project

- A 3D model for production of a new product project

- The design and layout of a client blueprint project

- The SEO of a web site

- The traffic / pay per click campaign for a web site

- A research project for cruise ship speaking

- A promotional animated video is in production

- All of my accounts, invoicing and book-keeping

So you can see there's a wide variety here.

Step 2 – Posting a Job

So how do you find someone to work for you? Well, in Elance jargon, you need to *post a job.*

How do you post a job? Click the green button called '*post your job*' and it's incredibly simple. For example, here's something I posted when I was looking for a traffic and SEO expert.

I put *Passionate about Traffic / Internet Marketing* as the job title. I then posted a quick job description. When doing a description I suggest you keep it brief but give it plenty of thought.

I try to emphasize three things in my Elance ads:

1. Talent

2. Experience

3. Culture

Here was the actual ad I posted.

Hello!

I'm looking for someone who is passionate about traffic, conversion and funnels. You'll know what there is to know about SEO, list management, mail outs, split testing, Google web master tools, analytics and more. You'll know about PPC on Google, FB and Amazon. You'll know how to leverage Kindle and penny traffic and a bunch of stuff beyond.

For you, sitting at a PC fiddling with funnels, membership sites and WordPress is second nature.

And, as a bonus, you're all kinds of good fun to work with. Life is too short, right?!

Looking forward to getting in touch,

Tim

That's a nice casual job ad. I think it's important to write these ads with your own style because that way people who like your style are drawn to you.

Let's look at some of the other things we need to specify.

- *Category of work.* This one went into the *sales and marketing* category. The sub categories were internet marketing and SEO. All the categories and sub categories are listed, so you just click on the ones that are suitable and follow the prompts.

- Next, I have to decide whether I want a **fixed price**. I decide I do. My budget is going to be less than $500.00. The great thing here is that allows other people to tell me what they think this job is worth. I don't set the price: they set the price and I get to choose the price that suits me best.

- As to further options, the one I like here is the **preferred location**. I get to choose someone from the region where I'm doing business. Anyone's welcome to apply but I'm looking for people in North America, for example.

- I can specify **how long** I want the job to be posted. In this case I posted the job for five days.

- Next, there's the **privacy option**. I can put the ad where everyone can see it and then I'll get lots of applications, but if I choose private, then only the people I invite to look at the application can see it.

- There are still other options. If I wanted to **pay extra**, I could get my job featured. I haven't used the featured option because I get plenty of replies so don't see the need to spend the extra cash on it. If I don't want that, I hit '*No thanks*'. Then I double-check everything and when it looks right, I hit '*Post*' and the job is online.

What's amazing is that this job now goes out to everybody who's searching for work. If the job is up for five days, I might come back to look tomorrow or I might wait until the listing closes. Then I look at the proposals job seekers have sent me. There will be a whole bunch. I scroll down and pick the ones that seem suitable for closer examination.

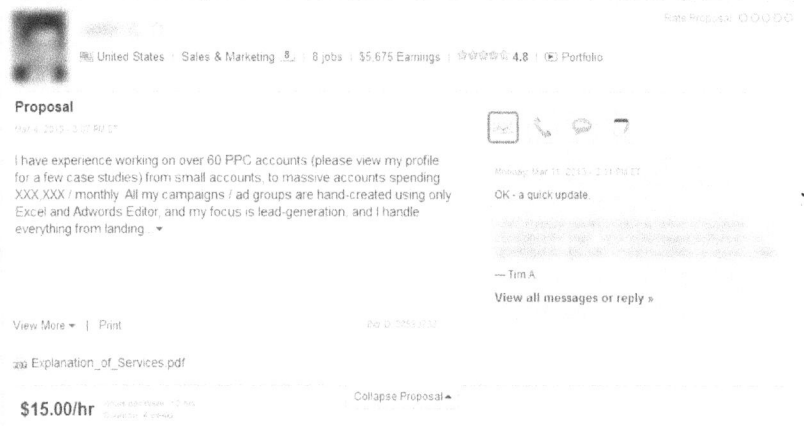

- To begin with, I check out the **location** of each proposal. I declined a few straight away because they weren't in

North America. I really wanted someone who knew the American turn of phrase for my content, so even though some of the hourly rates in India and some other places were down at $5 or $7 an hour, I rejected those offers. I looked closely at all the ones who specified they were in North America.

- To break down the selection process, I looked at the **ratings and references** from past clients. The person I actually selected had a rating of 8 out of 10 for sales and marketing as well as a referral rating 4.8 out of 5. That means people were very satisfied with his work.

- I looked at his **past earnings** through Elance too. That helps show how often he's worked in this system. My guy had earned $5,675. Other people had no ratings and no earnings.

- I also clicked on his **portfolio** to see some examples of previous work.

- The next step was to send him a message by email. I requested a **video call meeting** on Skype. This helps me make a decision. I always do the same thing when I'm picking someone through Elance. I choose the two or three people whose offers I like. Then I send a message to them saying let's talk on Skype. Even if I have the full profile of this person, with all their stats, a quick chat clarifies. I see if this person speaks the right sort of English, has the skill sets I want, and has the culture match for me.

- Once we were able to specify the job in more detail, he came back to me with a **real price** instead of a projected hourly rate. Even though he was working by the hour, I like to come to an agreement of the total hours *before* we begin.

Once I'm happy with the parameters, I press the green button marked 'Select', I fund the job and we're underway. Notice the money is not with the freelancer but with the Elance.com web site in escrow until I release it.

I make sure I see as many as possible on a video Skype call. I find this better aligns my personality and qualities with my freelancers. I have a rule to say I don't want anybody on my team who I don't look forward to talking to.

That might be a little bit too picky for some people. But I figure life's too short to be working with people I don't like. If I dread talking to them and think, "I'm going to be drained by this energy vampire again. I just hate dealing with this person," then I don't hire them. I hire freelancers who are terrific fun to talk to and offer a terrific project rate. You don't have to settle for someone you don't like because there are so many skilled workers when you open yourself up to a global labor force. You don't have to compromise your happiness or the entrepreneurial culture you're looking to create. There are tons of workers - which means you can choose one who fits well with you.

Step 4 – Hiring and Funding the Job

When I click 'Select', the website takes me through to the payment section, and it asks me to fund the job. The really great thing about Elance is if you put a payment in for a job, it puts your money in **escrow**. In other words, you're not paying the contractor directly, you're paying Elance. That way the contractor knows that the money is available to pay them, but they don't get it until the job is done to your satisfaction. Then you release it from Elance to the freelancer.

Elance is a very low risk way of getting work done piece by piece even on an ongoing basis. It's easy to find the people you need and the Elance system makes it a secure working environment.

Step 5 – Doing the Job

And that's pretty much it! Once you've found your freelancer, hired and funded them, you're in business. They work with you virtually to do the work you've specified until it's done.

If you're not totally satisfied with the job, and for whatever reason the contractor can't or won't fix the problem, then you can cancel the payment. Elance gives you your money back. Otherwise you can talk to Elance and raise what's termed a *dispute* if you have any problems.

Personally, I've never had any problems with this system. It's amazing!

It's a terrific place to resource your SEO needs *without* paying the premium associated with hiring an entire SEO Agency.

And that's the end of the excerpt from **the Entrepreneurial Handbook.**

 Not sure about outsourcing? Here's a link to a video I whipped up about Elance.com which will give you even more detail – http://www. timlevy.net/elance and a QR code to get you there.

FREQUENTLY
ASKED QUESTIONS

The Google Gamble

Frequently Asked Questions

As I've been writing this book, I've been working with a trusted group of beta-testers (thank you Anita, Chris, Robin, Barbara and Clint) to make sure it covers everything. From time to time, questions would come up that didn't fit directly in any particular part of the text. With that in mind, here are some helpful questions and answers to guide your traffic, content and SEO experience.

Is SEO a one-time thing?

Setting up your web site to be a structural match for SEO can happen just the one time. Once you have your web site loading quickly, error free and complete with the right pages (as specified in earlier chapters), then you're done for that particular issue.

However, good structure is simply a foundation. As you know by now, Google is engaged in an endless hunt for great content. Therefore, I'd be constantly feeding it with great, traffic-focused content. With that in mind, you'll constantly be coming up with ideas, then commissioning SEO research to find out if there's traffic for that idea. Once you have the right high-traffic, low-competition SEO keyword combination you can write your article and post it.

So do you need to pay someone to do constant SEO research? The answer is probably yes, if you're doing *constant content*. You'll need them to identify a series of high-traffic, low-competition keywords. The good news is that you can get it done on fiverr. com for $5. Those people might also help you by checking that your on-page SEO is good.

Do you need to pay someone to create constant backlinks and game Google? I would avoid that.

If you're generating constant content and promoting it appropriately – i.e. posting on Facebook and Twitter but not spamming, then I think you're doing fine. You might go further and see if someone will write a blog post pointing back to your awesome content. Perfect.

And again, I'd do all this in balance with four or five other experiments with other kinds of traffic. I'd focus on warmer traffic, for a start.

Once you've done all this, check Google Analytics. If your page is bringing traffic and converting, perfect. If it's not positively impacting your bottom line then I hate to say it, but it's a waste of time and money.

Can Graphic Designers do SEO as well?

I believe it takes different kinds of people to do left and right brain tasks. Design is an entirely right-brained and creative process. Creating content, for the most part, is a right-brain and creative process. SEO, in the other hand, is an entirely left-brained, logical and mathematical process. It's about endless research, tweaking parameters, rank tracking and traffic goals. It's about the math, it's all about the reports.

So have I seen a person who's a really talented designer who also does SEO? No. I haven't met that person yet. I tend to find one person who's good at each.

The SEO person tends to be – and this is a sweeping generalization here – buried in the computer. The SEO person usually loves living inside a computer and is constantly obsessing about the latest Google Panda updates.

A design person, on the other hand, is going to be talking to me about an amazing shade of gold that she is using on a header graphic. Designers are often also artists, so they're probably also painting or doing music.

The one person might have been able to master something like WordPress, but to be honest, probably not. Most good designers will give me Photoshop files and then leave me to get somebody else to code that into a WordPress theme.

So, I'm always hiring different people for their specialty, their focus. I never hire a designer to do SEO. I hire a designer, then a coder, then an SEO person. Or if it's an agency, I'll hire a design agency, a coding agency and then an SEO agency. I would be highly skeptical if the web designer said they'd do the SEO too.

And again, the nice thing about SEO is you can't lie about it. You can say "OK, show me some proof." If they don't show you a Google Analytics report or allow you to talk to a client of theirs, who tells you that it's working and they can track business back to it, I wouldn't hire them for SEO.

What about Sales Pages and Video Sales Letters?

When your traffic is really cold, as SEO traffic generally is, you may need to take extreme action to convert. This is why you'll see extra-long web pages making outrageous claims, with hard to believe testimonials, outrageous bonuses and over-the-top guarantees. Forgive if I'm repeating myself – this is definitely a personal soapbox moment. Another form of the same strategy is to create a video sales letter, characterized as black copy on a white background, with a voice-over reading the text.

There are lots of sales practices and marketing in the SEO industry that make me mad. Long form sales letters and video sales letters can really trigger me and it seems that I'm not alone.

I've noticed legitimate businesses – all I work with – *never* do this stuff.

An example of a legitimate business is one I'm doing some work with, an ad agency. If you go to their website you're going to see ads that they've done. Television, radio spots, print ads, beautiful design. You can see the clients they worked with, testimonials. They don't have on their front page a video-sales letter that is half an hour long, with a buy button 25 minutes in, trying to get you to do something. They don't have a long form sales letter that is 50 screens long, takes 25 minutes to read, that goes through the 12-step sales process.

They don't need to because they have something *genuine.*

If you're using a long form sales letter, it sets up an expectation that you're about to try to manipulate me into making a quick purchase. If you're trying to sell me 16 bonuses so I'm paying $97 for something worth $1,200, then I must ask "Why aren't I paying $1,200?"

Something Genuine

Apple is a great example. Apple has a policy of never discounting. If you go and buy an iPad, it's going to cost you $399 for the base model and that's it. They don't discount because they have a fantastic, legitimate product that everybody loves.

Apple never says 'This iPad comes with $1,200 of amazing bonuses, on offer *today only*. Click now!'

When a sales letter has *unreasonable* bonuses or guarantees – I tend to think the whole thing is a scam.

Of course, I freely admit that this is just my particular soapbox. I'm not trying to say that every sales letter, or video sales letter, is bad, because they're not. There's some brilliant stuff out there, but for me as a consumer, if I see things that are too good to be true, I believe they are too good to be true. So I don't buy them.

None of my clients try to sell you with unreasonable promises and stupid bonuses and crazy guarantees, because *they don't need to.* They deliver genuine value established over time.

What is Split Testing?

Split testing is when you create two webpages that have a similar offer, send traffic to both to find out which one gets you better results. Split testing is a technique that allows you to experiment to find the optimal conversion for a particular page or offer. Most often you split test one variable at a time such as a particular headline, maybe a button size, layout option or color.

That's the great thing about the web – everything comes back to measurable results. It's not like putting an ad in a magazine, where it's hard to measure the results. With a print ad, for example, you run the ad, you sit back and cross your fingers, watching your sales and hoping for a blip to coincide with the ad campaign.

With split testing, you don't have to hope. The process of tracking your cursor, clicking a buy or call to action button and tracking goals is measurable and free via Google Analytics.

PUTTING IT ALL TOGETHER

The Google Gamble

Putting It All Together

So there you have it – traffic, conversion and SEO. Here's the salient summary.

i. SEO, which I call the Google Gamble, is designed to bring raw traffic to your web site.

ii. It's a gamble because Google doesn't share the specifics of its algorithm: you must guess.

iii. It's one of many ways to generate traffic, or raw business leads, for your business.

iv. The practical steps of SEO involve trying to make your

site into something that Google's algorithm will favor. There are four key steps –

a. Step 1 – Shaping your web site

b. Step 2 – Finding relevant traffic

c. Step 3 – Creating genuine and valuable content

d. Step 4 – Tracking your results

v. You can do it yourself, train an internal team or outsource the whole deal via sites like fiverr.com and elance.com.

Done right, you'll have a web site awash with raw traffic. At that point it's all about *conversion* - the art and science of moving someone from being a *potential* to an *actual* paying customer. For that, we're going to need another book!

What are the basic steps, one more time?

Preparation

First, make sure your website is tied to Google Analytics, if not something like it. Otherwise it's like trying to walk across a busy road with your eyes closed. It's crazy. So open your eyes first, and to do that, you need an active Google Analytics account.

With that, you can make good decisions about all your traffic, SEO included.

Check your Google Analytics and ask yourself seriously, does your company even need SEO? Honestly, it's one of 10 tools I use for traffic and it's not my favorite, because it's such a gamble. That's the key point of this book. SEO is not my first choice for traffic. It's not even appropriate for lots of businesses. I'm working with a business right now and 90-percent of their traffic comes from physical road signage, so why would I spend all this time on SEO when I could spend it optimizing my signs?

Step One - Structure

Second, commission a quick assessment of your site and the traffic it already has. If you need structural changes, make them.

One site I recently worked on had set its meta-tags to say "Please ignore me, Google" and didn't even know. Get your foundations right. Hire an SEO Agency or professional to do it for you.

Step Two – Traffic

Begin a set of four or five traffic experiments, of which SEO is merely one. With regard to the SEO, commission the research that shows there is traffic potential for the pages on your site.

Step Three - Content

Once you have high-traffic low-competition keywords, begin to create a never-ending stream of awesome content to match it.

What do you have to have? The answers is simple, you must have great content. This is what we've said from the first part of this book to the last. Google is doing its best to find genuine great content. So have great content.

If your website is just a brochure, that's not great content. Great content is something that people will stop to read, then like, then share with their friends. If that isn't happening, try again! From experience, Google wants you to be the best answer to a question in a genuine way, so make sure you are the best answer.

Step Four – Measure

Once you have great content, be sure Google knows about it by putting your sitemap through Google Web Master Tools. Measure the traffic. Use Google Analytics to see if your page is ranking and getting hits. Once it's getting hits, be sure to assess whether that traffic is generating actions that lead to new business.

Once you've mastered those steps, you'll have something real that will grow and sustain your business over time. Nothing less will do.

END WORD +
BONUSES

The Google Gamble

End Word + Bonuses

There's a wonderful book I truly love called *Illusions* by Richard Bach. At the very end, he writes

> *'Everything*
>
> *in this book*
>
> *may be*
>
> *wrong.'*

That's the hilarious joke behind SEO: in the end it's all well intentioned *guesswork*. Google is constantly tweaking its algorithm. What works today may not work tomorrow. As I stated at the very beginning, SEO is a wonderful and amusing gamble. As with gambling, you would never put all your eggs in one basket, your money on one bet. As with gambling, you would never grumble if it didn't pay off. You play the odds over time and hope for the best.

A good, solid traffic strategy designed to bring lots of customers to your site will include SEO as merely *one of many tactics.*

In addition to that, some businesses are a great match for SEO and some aren't. Remember that Google traffic is raw, cold traffic. You still have to convert people from never having met you to actual, paying customers.

So best of luck in your endless game of find the customer, get the customer, keep the customer. I hope this book has helped bring some perspective to the traffic, content and SEO pieces of the puzzle, debunking some of the myths while bringing you clarity, new strategies and the tools to implement them.

The Bigger Picture

I don't pretend to be the world's foremost expert on the latest permutations of SEO. To be honest, there are geekier, nerdier people out there by far. These people spend endless hours on a computer staying up to date and in practice with the hottest SEO techniques out there.

I don't even pretend to do that, nor would I want to.

Instead, I spend my days as a writer, speaker, coach and consultant to the CEOs of genuine businesses. I favor businesses that are focused *beyond the dollar* on things that are meaningful, intentional and bring a little something extra to the world. My goal is to make a tangible, measurable difference to each and every one of these businesses. Together we build strategies that guide these businesses to genuine and effective growth over the course of months, years and beyond.

My perspective on SEO, then, fits into that bigger picture. Together with the CEO, I weigh the costs and benefits of a range of traffic, conversion and product tactics to maximize growth and minimize risk at the same time. We shape that into an overall blueprint which is then implemented over time. This brings the most consistent, grounded results possible.

This is what I'm committed to and I highly recommend the same for you.

Bonus / Driving Traffic

It's now six or twelve months *after* I wrote the original version of the Google Gamble and I've learned a thing or two. While lots of people love the idea of building a solid SEO web site, others would like to know about other, *less-risky* and *more direct* methods of driving traffic.

With that in mind, I've created a couple of videos which you're free to check out online.

Sneaky Method One

Here's a link to a video on driving traffic inexpensively through social media. For example, using this neat method just once, my business wound up in front of over 27,000 people, engaged 580 of them directly and drove 121 of them to web site for just over $20. Interesting, right?

 Here's a link to that video - http://www.timlevy. net/facebook or a QR code to get you there.

**Sneaky Method Two**

Here's a second video about driving traffic through a totally different method. This is another method that you can use to conduct traffic experiments that begins at around $10 or $20 each, delivering your message to audiences of tens of thousands of interested people.

 Here's a link to that video – http://www.timlevy.net/ads or a QR code to get you there.

Bonus / 100% SEO

Another question I've been frequently asked is _How do you know when your SEO is done?_

Well, while you cannot ever be _done_ with the SEO that happens beyond your site, you can be _100% done_ with SEO on any given page. There are a series of neat little plugins for your browser that allow you to check that.

The one I like is a free plugin for the Firefox browser called SEO Doctor. It gives every web page a rating out of 100% as you browse the web, going _green_ when you have a 100% rating. So you can check your web site by simply looking for green flags. In the event that the flag is yellow, orange or red, SEO

Doctor will tell you what is lacking.

I have my SEO team continue working on a site until the SEO Doctor gives each individual page a 100% rating, then I'm done!

 Here's a link to the SEO Doctor –http://www. timlevy.net/seodoctor or a QR code to get you there.

About the Author

Tim Levy is an author, speaker, consultant and coach. He works with CEOs and entrepreneurs on clarity, strategy and mindset. He routinely speaks for peak organizations like Vistage International, CEOSpace International and Secret Knock. He has a particular focus on web technology and digital content including books, CDs, online training and broadcast television. His clients report transformational shifts and rapid growth in their business and personal lives.

He's available via his web site at www.timlevy.net.

Other Recent Titles Include ..

Available online at www.timlevy.net

Tim Levy

Clarity is everything.

Home   About Tim Levy ▾   Coaching ▾   Writing ▾   Speaking ▾   Blog ▾   Training ▾   Contact ▾

Enter our Great Radio Competition Giveaway.

Clarity – Strategy – Mindset

Tim Levy is an author, speaker, consultant and coach working with CEOs and entrepreneurs on clarity, strategy and mindset. I routinely speak for leading organizations like Vistage International, CEOSpace International and Secret Knock. Furthermore my clients consistently report transformational shifts and rapid growth in their business and personal lives.

'And one more thing – I focus on businesses that are focused beyond the dollar on things that are meaningful, intentional and bring a little something extra to the world.'

Through this work I've created a a unique skill set and combination of services specifically tailored to those looking for more meaning in their business and life.

Here is a quick look at our latest video on YouTube. You can always join our free newsletter to have one delivered to your inbox every 2-4 weeks. Enjoy!

Coaching	**Writing**	**Speaking**	**Shopping**
Coaching CEOs and entrepreneurs to radical shifts and startling leaps in their business and personal lives.	All my clarity, strategy and mindset concepts, tools and processes in a series of best-selling books.	Speaking across America for peak organizations like Vistage, CEOSpace and Secret Knock	Online training courses, DVDs, CDs and books that make a significant difference in your business and personal lives.

Please visit me at www.timlevy.net

Is there more I can do?

If there is any way I can help you further, then let's talk. Please call, email me directly or via *Contact Us* on the site, and I'll see what I can do.

Tim Levy and Associates LLC

Based In | Austin, Texas

Telephone | (512) 782 4401

Email | creativity@timlevy.net

Web | www.timlevy.net

www.ingramcontent.com/pod-product-compliance
Lightning Source LLC
Chambersburg PA
CBHW051714170526
45167CB00002B/662